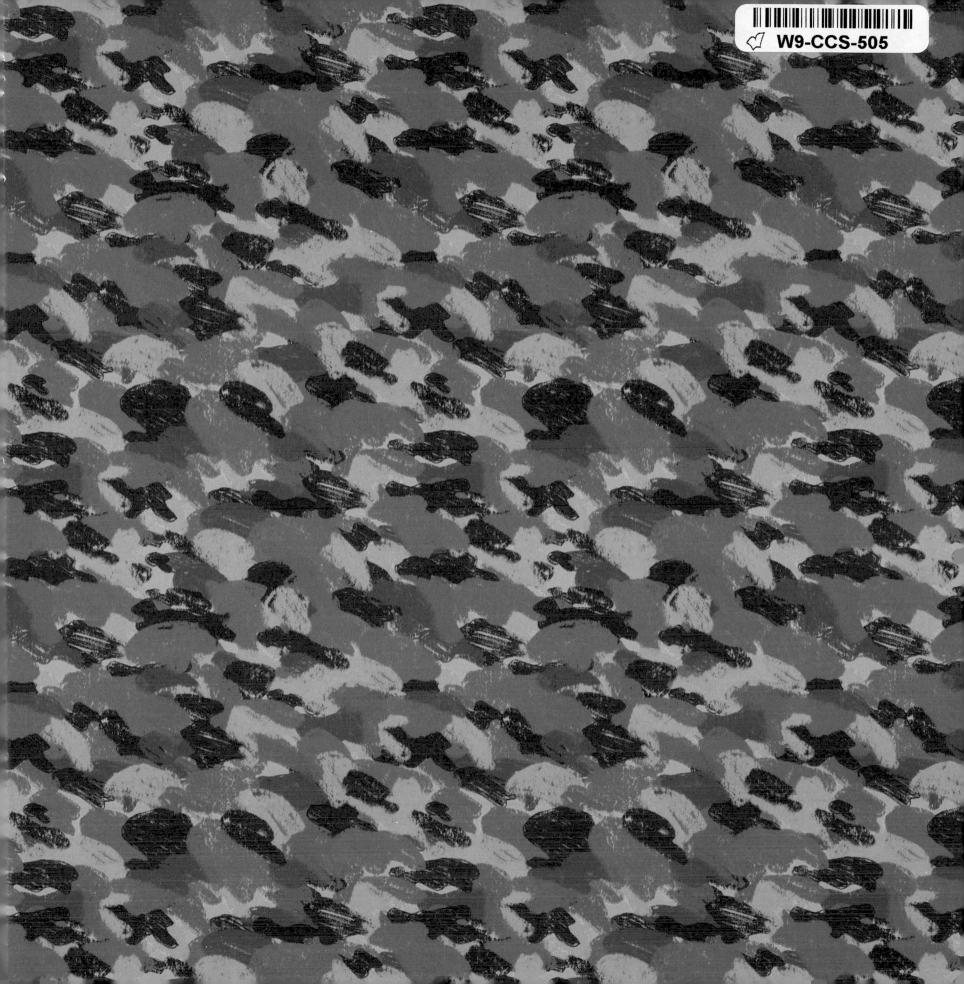

For Mum

H.T.

With thanks to Renee, for her invaluable
suggestions, and for her service.

First American Edition 2018
Kane Miller, A Division of EDC Publishing
PO Box 470663, Tulsa, OK 74147-0663
www.kanemiller.com
Text by Isabel Otter
Text copyright © Caterpillar Books 2018
Illustrations copyright © Hannah Tolson 2018
Library of Congress Control Number: 2017948140
978-1-61067-721-9
Printed in China
CPB/1400/0823/1217
10 9 8 7 6 5 4 3 2 1

My Mommy is a Hero

Illustrated by *hannah tolson*

Kane Miller
A DIVISION OF EDC PUBLISHING

My mommy is a hero;
courageous, strong, inspired.

She keeps the
peace and
protects us;

for this she is admired.

My mommy is a hero,

her strength amazes me.

She dives into the ocean,
to rescue those at sea.

My mommy is a hero,
she helps to train cadets.

Under her great leadership
they always pass the test!

My mommy is a hero,
she jumps from planes on high.

I think she watches over me
from far up in the sky.

My mommy is a hero,
leading others every day.

I know she's always with me,
even when she's far away.

My mommy is a hero,

a dog handler supreme!

With her support and training,
they're all part of the team.

My mommy is a hero,
she flies from land to sea.

I love her and look up to her,
she's always guiding me.

My mommy is a hero,
she's passionate
and smart.

I know she works to keep us safe;
I hold her in my heart.

My mommy is a hero,

she travels far and wide.

She serves with so much bravery,
and I am full of pride.

My mommy is a hero, she helps people in need.

Always putting others first,
we all follow her lead.

My mommy is a hero,

she's a pilot without fear.

Her missions take her round the world
to countries far and near.

My mommy is a hero;

courageous, strong, inspired.

She keeps the peace and protects us;
for this she is admired.

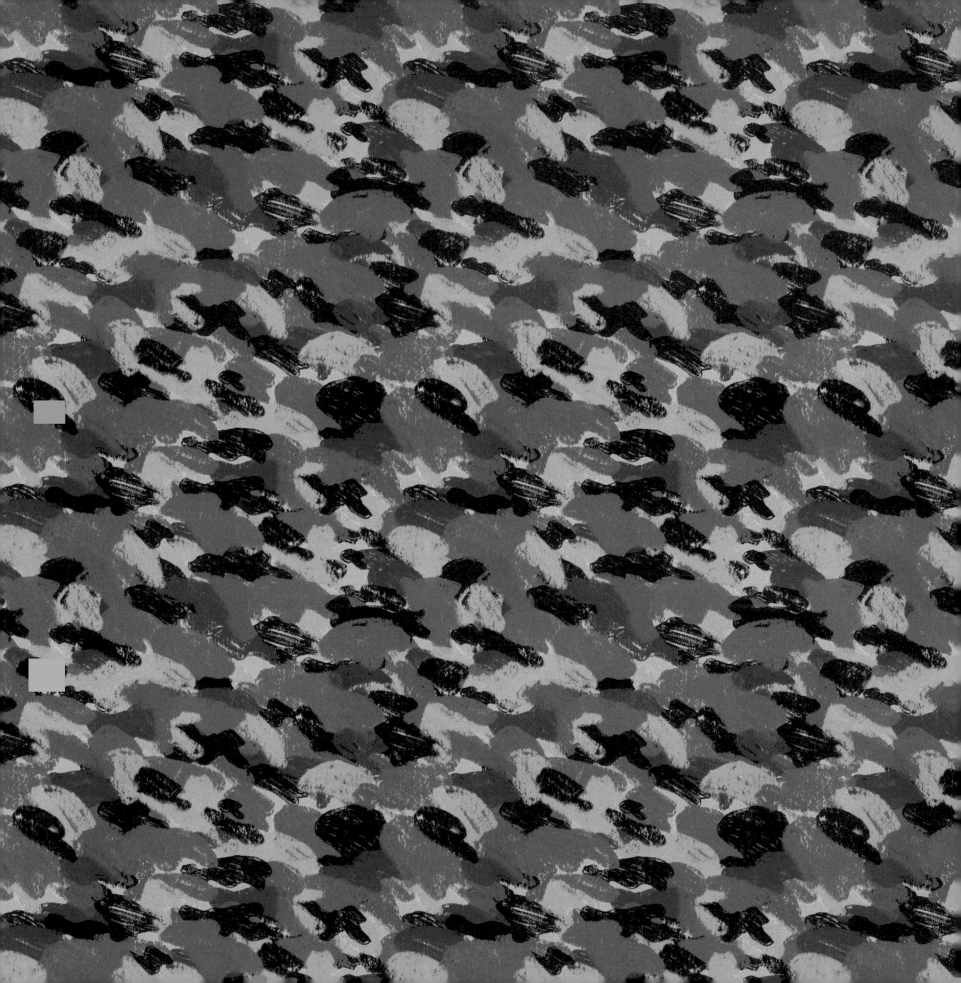